Jenny Cockina

CW00525939

The New Novello Choral Edition

LUDWIG VAN BEETHOVI

Missa solemnis
(*Mass in D*)
Op.123

for soprano, alto, tenor and bass soli, SATB and orchestra

handwritten annotations:
Terrace Lounge US Be there 2.30.
28ᵗʰ Feb. Tues. 7.30. St Lawrence.
Do Gloria p39
Credo wed: week re.
25.1.06 p100
30ᵗʰ April 7.30

Revised by Michael Pilkington

Order No: NOV 072497

NOVELLO PUBLISHING LIMITED
8/9 Frith Street, London, W1V 5TZ

It is requested that on all concert notices and programmes acknowledgement is made to 'The New Novello Choral Edition'.

Es wird gebeten, auf sämtlichen Konzertankündigungen und Programmen 'The New Novello Choral Edition' als Quelle zu erwähnen.

Il est exigé que toutes les notices et programmes de concerts, comportent des remerciements à 'The New Novello Choral Edition'.

Cover illustration: first vocal entry in the 'Kyrie eleison' of Beethoven's *Missa solemnis* from Schott's 1827 edition.

© Copyright 1999 Novello & Company Limited.

Published in Great Britain by Novello Publishing Limited
Head office: 8/9 Frith Street, LONDON, W1V 5TZ
Tel +44 (0)171 434 0066   Fax +44 (0)171 287 6329

Sales and Hire: Music Sales Distribution Centre,
Newmarket Road, Bury St Edmunds, Suffolk IP33 3YB
Tel +44 (0)1284 702600   Fax +44 (0)1284 768301

Web: www.internetmusicshop.com   e-mail: music@musicsales.co.uk

All Rights reserved   Printed in Great Britain

No part of this publication may be copied or reproduced in any form or by any means without the prior permission of Novello & Company Limited.

Ohne vorherige Genehmigung der Firma Novello & Company Limited darf kein Bestandteil dieser Publikation in irgendeiner Form oder auf irgendeine Art und Weise kopiert bzw. reproduziert werden.

Aucune partie de cette publication ne pourra être copiée ni reproduite sous quelque forme que ce soit, ni par quelque moyen que ce soit, sans l'autorisation préalable de Novello & Company Limited.

PREFACE

This revision is based on the first edition, 1827 (**A**) and the Gesamtausgabe published by Breitkopf & Härtel in the 1860s (**B**). The (uncredited) accompaniment in the old Novello edition has been modified to conform more closely with the full score. The inconsistent slurring of the voice parts is from the sources. Textual inconsistencies have been resolved by reference to the current approved spelling and punctuation of the Mass text, as found in the *Missal in Latin and English* (Burns, Oates and Washbourne, 1950). All editorial additions are shown by strokes through slurs or hairpins, or by placing within square brackets.

NOTES

CREDO, bb. 124-131: The first phrase of 'Et incarnatus' is given to the chorus tenors in the autograph, to the solo tenor in **A**, but to the chorus in **B**. The use of the soloist may well be Beethoven's final decision; on the other hand the accompaniment is only reduced to single strings at bar 132, where the solo alto takes over the vocal line. Tovey[1] prefers the use of chorus tenors, while Hess[2] gives the phrase to the soloist. See Drabkin for further information[3].

SANCTUS: "The voice parts of the 'Pleni sunt cæli' and 'Osanna' are assigned to the solo quartet in the primary sources, as in the first edition (and in all subsequent editions)."[4] According to Hess, Beethoven later told Schindler "They must be solo voices"[5]. However, it is almost impossible for solo voices to be heard above the full orchestra. Drabkin makes it clear that the autograph is ambiguous at this point: only four staves are used for the voices in the 'Sanctus', whereas eight were needed in the 'Credo', and throughout the 'Sanctus' the lowest four staves are left blank. Beethoven did not specifiy whether he meant solo or chorus for the 'Sanctus'. The most practical solution would seem to be to use soloists for the 'Sanctus', and chorus for the 'Pleni sunt cæli' and 'Osanna' as given in the old Novello edition.

AGNUS DEI, bb. 181-185: All sources, and the present edition, give this passage for flutes and bassoons thus, in spite of the violent clash between bassoon its accompaniment:

Though in his notes Hess suggests that the dissonance may be intentional, as in the famous passage at the point of recapitulation in the first movement of the *Eroica*, Breitkopf & Härtel and Eulenberg solve the problem thus:

Peters has:

Michael Pilkington
Old Coulsdon, February 1999

1   Donald Francis Tovey: Beethoven: *Missa Solemnis*, Op. 123, *Essays in Musical Analysis*, vol. V (London 1937), p.172.
2   Beethoven: *Missa Solemnis*, ed. Willy Hess, (London c. 1964) [Eulenberg miniature score], p.xi.
3   William Drabkin: *Beethoven: Missa Solemnis* (Cambridge 1991), p.23.
4   Ibid. p.24
5   Hess, op. cit. p.v.

NOTE

This revised edition of the *Mass in D (Missa solemnis)* follows the layout of the previous edition (catalogue number NOV070049) page for page, to allow this new edition to be used side-by-side with the edition it supersedes.

MISSA SOLEMNIS
(Mass in D)

KYRIE ELEISON

© Copyright 1999 Novello & Company Limited

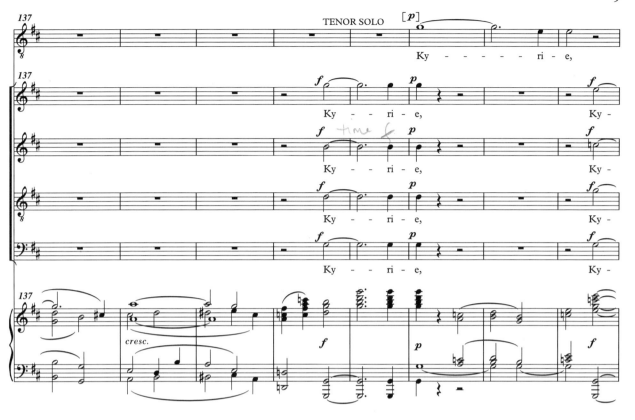

11

GLORIA IN EXCELSIS

20

184
fff
De - us pa - ter om - - - - - - - - -
pa - ter om - - - - - - - - -
De - us pa - ter om - - - - - - - - -
pa - ter om - - - - - - - - -
189
- ni - - po - tens.
sf
dim.
194
SOPRANO SOLO [p]
Do -
TENOR SOLO [p]
Do - mi-ne fi - li u - - ni - ge - ni - te,
BASS SOLO [p]
Do - mi-ne fi - li u - - ni - ge - ni - te,
p

25

28

Quo - ni - am tu so - lus sanc - tus.

Quo - ni - am tu so - lus Do - - - mi - nus.

40

44

52

CREDO

62

ET INCARNATUS

* See Preface

ET RESURREXIT

SANCTUS *

* See Preface

*See Preface

PRELUDIUM

BENEDICTUS

CHORUS
BASS
Be - ne - dic - tus qui ve - nit in no - mi - ne
Do - mi - ni.

dolce cantabile

espressivo

112

AGNUS DEI

DONA NOBIS

D **Allegretto vivace** Bitte um innern und äussern Frieden

148

Printed and bound in Great Britain by
Caligraving Limited Thetford Norfolk
10/04 (52885)